AF407541

Hex codes, or hexadecimal codes, are a way to represent colors in digital devices and web design. Each hex code refers to a very specific color. A hex color is expressed as a six-digit combination of numbers and letters, preceded by a pound sign or hashtag, defined by its mix of red, green, and blue (RGB). The first two letters or numbers refer to red, the next two refer to green, and the last two refer to blue.

The color values are defined as values between 00 and FF. Hex codes are a universal way to describe colors. This book is specifically about earth tones.

A is for artichoke

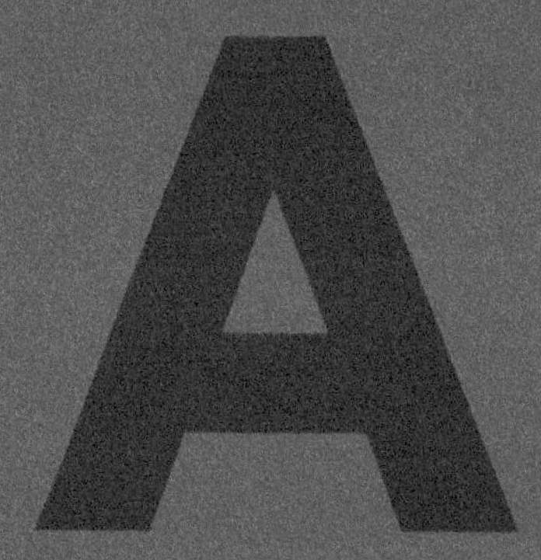

#4B6D41

a is for auburn

a

#712F2C

B is for blue lagoon

B

#00626F

b is for blue paisley

b

#2282A8

C is for charcole grey

#6E6969

c is for charred clay

c

#885132

E is for earth brown

E

#4F1507

e is for evergreen forest

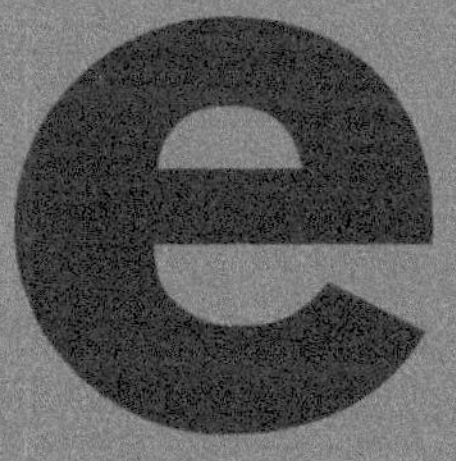

#0E695F

F is for forest floor

#555142

f is for forest night

f

#434237

G is for glacier grey

G

#C5C6C7

g is for grey wolf

g

#9CA0A6

H is for handmade

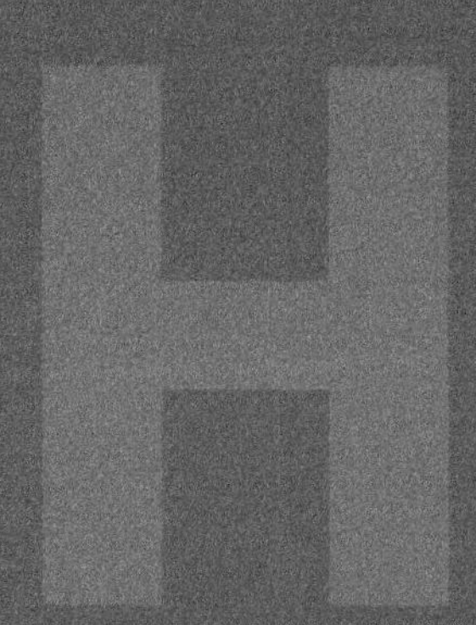

#7F735F

h is for hemp

h

#987D73

I is for iko iko

I

#B3AB6E

i is for irish clover

#53734C

J is for jacko bean

J

#2E1905

j is for jasmine flower

j

#F4E8E1

K is for kelp

K

#454936

k is for kelp forest

k

#448811

M is for meltwater

M

#79C0CC

m is for moss green

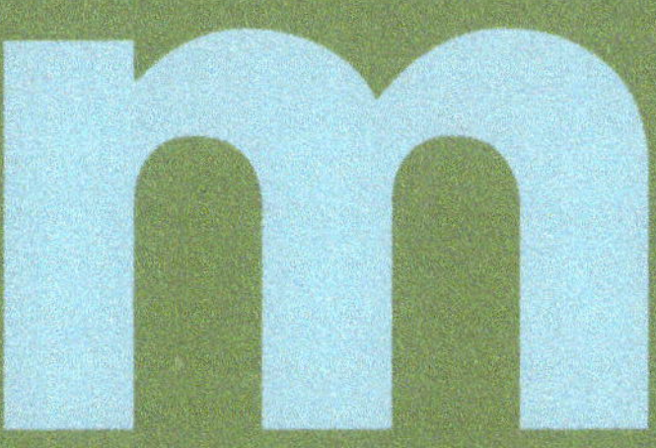

#638B27

N is for niagara blue

N

#5E849D

n is for nut brown

n

#5A3826

O is for ocher

#BF9B0C

o is for orange lily

#BE7249

P is for peaslake

P

#8CAA95

p is for prairie dusk

p

#CEC5AD

Q is for quartz smoky

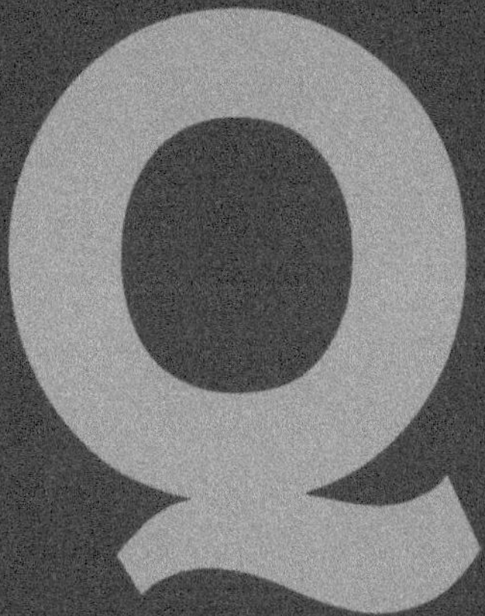

#51484F

q is for quicksand

q

#BD978E

R is for rolling sea

R

#5A6D77

r is for rust

r

#A83C09

S is for seagrass

S

#67AD83

s is for straw yellow

S

#F0D696

T is for tumbleweed

T

#37290E

t is for turtle lake

#73B7A5

U is for umber

U

#635147

u is for underwater

u

#0C2766

V is for vanilla

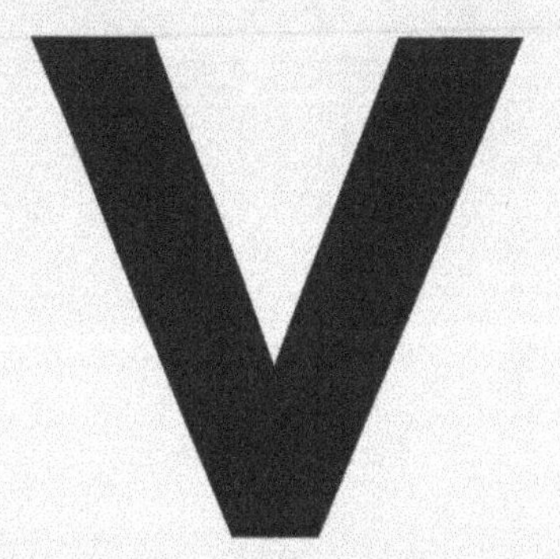

#F3EAB0

v is for vintage violet

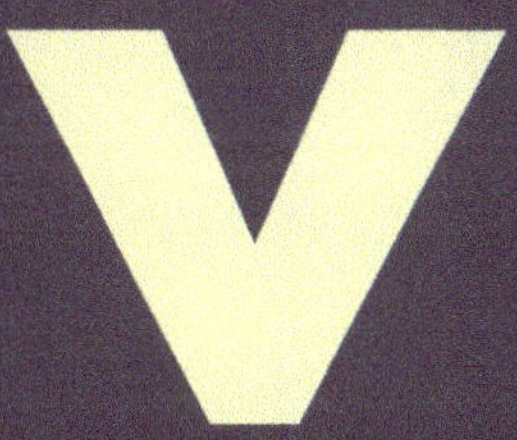

#634F62

W is for waterfall

#3AB0A2

w is for waterway

w

#7EB7BF

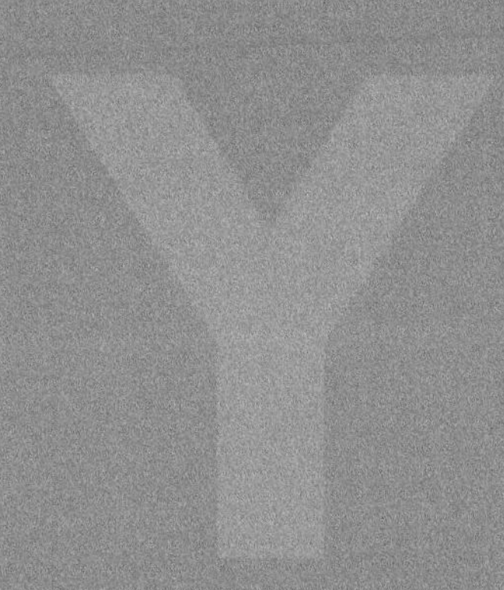
Y is for yam
Y
#CC6600

y is for yamabukicha

#CB7E1F

Z is for zen garden

#C7CFA2

z is for zenith

z

#95B9E1